BOOKS BY RITA DOVE

The Yellow House on the Corner (poems, 1980)

Museum (poems, 1983)

Fifth Sunday (short stories, 1985)

Thomas and Beulah (poems, 1986)

Grace Notes (poems, 1989)

Through the Ivory Gate (novel, 1992)

Selected Poems (1993)

The Darker Face of the Earth (verse drama, 1994)

Mother Love (poems, 1995)

The Poet's World (essays, 1995)

On the Bus with Rosa Parks (poems, 1999)

On the Bus with Rosa Parks

Poems

Rita Dove

W. W. Norton & Company

New York • London

For information about permission to reproduce selections from this
book, write to Permissions, W. W. Norton & Company, Inc.,
500 Fifth Avenue, New York, NY 10110.

The text of this book is composed in Sabon
with the display set in Univers
Desktop composition by Julia Druskin
Manufacturing by Courier Companies, Inc.
Book design by BTD

Library of Congress Cataloging-in-Publication Data

Dove, Rita.
On the bus with Rosa Parks : poems / Rita Dove.
p.   cm.
ISBN 0-393-04722-9
1. Afro-American women civil rights workers—Poetry. 2. Civil rights
movements—United States—Poetry. 3. Afro-Americans—Civil rights—
Poetry. 4. Afro-American women—Poetry. I. Title.
PS3554.0884052   1999
811'.54—dc21   98-45057
CIP

ISBN 0-393-32026-X pbk.

W. W. Norton & Company, Inc., 500 Fifth Avenue, New York, N.Y. 10110
http://www.wwnorton.com

W. W. Norton & Company Ltd., 10 Coptic Street, London WC1A 1PU

1 2 3 4 5 6 7 8 9 0

for
Aviva

for
Fred

Contents

Revenant

On the Bus with Rosa Parks

Cameos

Cameos

July, 1925

Lucille among the flamingos
is pregnant; is pained
because she cannot stoop to pluck
the plumpest green tomato
deep on the crusted vine.
Lucille considers
the flamingos, guarding in plastic cheer
the birdbath, parched
and therefore
deserted. In her womb
a dull—no, a husky ache.

If she picks it, Joe will come home
for breakfast tomorrow.
She will slice and dip it
in egg and cornmeal and fry
the tart and poison out.
Sobered by the aroma, he'll show
for sure, and sit down
without a mumbling word.
Inconsiderate, then,

the vine that languishes
so!, and the bath sighing for water
while the diffident flamingos arrange
their torchsong tutus.
She alone
is the blues. Pain drives her blank.

Lucille thinks: *I can't*
even see my own feet.

Lucille lies down
between tomatoes
and the pole beans: heavenly shade.
From here everything looks
reptilian. The tomato plops
in her outstretched palm. *Now*
he'll come, she thinks,
and it will be a son.
The birdbath hushes
behind a cloud
of canebreak and blossoming flame.

N i g h t

Joe ain't studying *nobody.*
He laughs his own sweet bourbon banner,
he makes it to work on time.
Late night, Joe retreats through
the straw-link-and-bauble curtain
and up to bed. Joe sleeps. Snores
gently as a child after a day of marbles.

Joe
knows somewhere
he had a father
who would have told him
how to act. Mama,
stout as a yellow turnip,
loved to bewail her wild good luck:
Blackfoot Injun, tall with
hair like a whip. Now

to do it
without him
is the problem. To walk into a day
and quietly absorb.
Joe takes after Mama.
Joe's Mr. Magoo.
Joe
thinks, half
dreaming, if he ever finds
a place where he can think,
he'd stop clowning
and drinking and then that wife
of his would quit
sending prayers through the chimney.

Ah,
Lucille.
Those eyes, bright and bitter
as cherry bark, those
coltish shins, those thunderous hips!
No wonder he couldn't leave
her be, no wonder whenever she began to show
he packed a fifth and split.

Joe
in funk and sorrow. Joe
in parkbench celibacy, in apostolic
factory rote, in guilt (the brief
astonishment of memory), in grief when
guilt turns monotonous.

He always knows when to go on home.

Birth

(So there you are at last—
a pip, a button in the grass.
The world's begun
without you.

And no reception but
accumulated time.
Your face hidden but your name
shuddering on air!)

Lake Erie Skyline, 1 9 3 0

He lunges, waits, then strikes again.
I'll make them sweat, he thinks
and does a spider dance
as the fireflies shamble past.

The sky dims slowly; the sun
prefers to do its setting
on the other side of town.
This deeper blue smells
soft. The patterns in it
rearrange—he cups

another fly. (He likes to
shake them dizzy
in his hands, like dice, then
throw them out for luck.
They blink on helplessly
then stagger from the sidewalk
up and gone.)

Sometimes the night arrives
with liquor on its breath,
twice-rinsed and chemical.
Or hopped up, sparking
a nervous shimmy. Or
dangerously still, like his mother
standing next to the stove,
a Bible verse rousing her pursed lips.

He knows what gin is made from—
berries blue. He knows
that Jesus Saves. (His father
calls it Bitches' Tea.)

And sisters—so many, their
names fantastic, myriad
as the points of a chandelier:
Corinna, Violet, Mary, Fay,
Suzanna, Kit, and Pearl. Each evening
when they came to check
his bed, he held his breath, and still
he smelled the camphor
and hair pomade. Saw
foreheads sleek, spitcurl
embellishing a cheek, lips
soft and lashes spiked
with vaseline. He waited
to be blessed.
        They were
Holy Vessels, Mother said:
each had to wait
her Turn. And he, somehow,
was part of the waiting, he was
the chain. He was, somehow,
his father.
. . .

The latest victim won't
get up—just lies there
in the middle of the walk
illuminating the earth
regular as breath.
He stomps and grinds
his anger in. Pulls
his foot away and yellow
streaks beneath the sole—
eggyolk flame, lurid
smear of sin.

　　　　Sisters,
laughing, take his shoes away
and bring them scraped
and ordinary
back. *Idiots,*
he thinks. *No wonder
there's so many of them.*

But he can't sleep.
All night beneath his bed,
the sun is out.

Depression Years

　　　　　　　　Pearl
　　　　　can't stop eating;
　　　　　she wants to live!
　　　　　Those professors
　　　　have it all backwards:
　　　after fat came merriment,
　　simply because she was afraid to
　　face the world, its lukewarm

nonchalance
that generationwise had set
her people in a stupor of
religion and
gambling debts. (Sure, her
mother was an angel
but her daddy was
her man.)

Pearl laughs
a wet red laugh.
Pearl oozes
everywhere. When she was
young, she licked the walls free of chalk; she
ate dust for the minerals.
Now she just
enjoys, and excess
hardens on her like
a shell.
She sheens.

But oh, what
tiny feet! She tipples
down the stairs. She cracks a chair.
The largest baby shoe
is neat. Pearl laughs
when Papa jokes: *Why don't*
you grow yourself some feet?
Her mother calls them
devil's hooves.
Her brother
doesn't

care.
He has
A Brain; he doesn't notice.
She gives him of her own
ham hock, plies him with
sweetened yams. Unravels
ratted sweaters, reworks them
into socks. In the lean years
lines his shoes
with newspaper. *(Main
thing is, you don't
miss school.)*

She tells him
it's the latest style.
He never laughs.
He reads. He
shuts her out.
Pearl thinks
she'll never marry—
though she'd
like to have
a child.

Homework

"The Negro and his song
are inseparable.
If his music is primitive
and if it has much that
is sensuous, this is simply
a part of giving
pleasure, a quality
appealing strongly
to the Negro's

entire being. Indeed,
his love of rhythms
and melody, his
childish faith
in dreams . . ."
Shit,
he'll take Science, most
Exacting Art.
In school when the teacher
makes him lead
the class in song,
he'll cough straight through.
Better
columns of figures, the thing
dissected to the bone.
Better
the clear and incurious *drip*
of fluid from pipet
to reassuring beaker.
"The Negro claps his hands
spontaneously; his feet
move constantly in joyful
anticipation of the drum. . . ."
Most of all
he'd like to study
the composition of the stars.

Graduation, Grammar School

Joe
holds both
fists out, palms
down. *Come on boy, guess.*

The boy
hesitates. He knows
there's nothing
in either one.
(The game:
Who offers the hand
first, man or woman?
Who first lowers
the eyes? If the hand
is not received, whose
price is reduced? And
what if both are men?
Or drunk? Or one is
white? The possibilities
are infinite.)

Joe
sees his son
flicker. Although
the air is not a glass,
watches as he puts his lips to
the brim—then turns away, bored.
He is not mine, this son
who ripens, quiet
poison on a
shelf.

Painting the Town

The mirror
in the hall is red.
Pearl
giggles: *Pretty*
as a freshly painted

barn. She tugs
a wrinkle down.
Since she's discovered
men would rather drown
than nibble,
she does just
fine.

She'd like to show
her brother
what it is like to crawl
up the curved walls
of the earth, or
to be that earth—but
he has other plans.
Which is alright. Which is
As It Should Be.
Let the boy reach manhood
anyway he can.

Easter Sunday, 1940

A purity
in sacrifice, a blessedness
in shame. Lucille
in full regalia, clustered
violets and crucifix.
She shoos
a hornet
back to Purgatory,
rounds the corner, finds
her son in shirtsleeves staring

from the porch into the yard
as if it were the sea.

And suddenly
she doesn't care.
(Joe, after all, came home.)
She feels as if
she's on her back
again, and all around her
blushing thicket.

Nightwatch. The Son.

(Aggressively adult,
they keep their
lives, to which
I am a witness.

At the other end
I orbit, pinpricked
light. I watch.
I float and grieve.)

Freedom:
Bird's-Eye View

Singsong

When I was young, the moon spoke in riddles
and the stars rhymed. I was a new toy
waiting for my owner to pick me up.

When I was young, I ran the day to its knees.
There were trees to swing on, crickets for capture.

I was narrowly sweet, infinitely cruel,
tongued in honey and coddled in milk,
sunburned and silvery and scabbed like a colt.

And the world was already old.
And I was older than I am today.

I Cut My Finger Once on Purpose

I'm no baby. There's no grizzly man
wheezing in the back of the closet.
When I was the only one,
they asked me if I wanted a night-light
and I said *yes*—
but then came the shadows.

I know they make the noises at night.

My toy monkey Giselle, I put her
in a red dress they said was mine
once—but if it was mine, why did they yell
when Giselle clambered up the porch maple
and tore it? Why would Mother say
*When you grow up, I hope you have
a daughter just like you*

if it weren't true, that I *have* a daughter
hidden in the closet—someone
they were ashamed of and locked away
when I was too small to cry.

I watch them all the time now:
Mother burned herself at the stove
without wincing. Father
smashed a thumb in the Ford,
then stuck it in his mouth for show.
They bought my brother a just-for-boys
train, so I grabbed the caboose
and crowned him—but he toppled

from his rocker without a bleat;
he didn't even bleed.

That's when I knew they were
robots. But I'm no idiot:
I eat everything they give me,
I let them put my monkey away.
When I'm big enough
I'll go in, past the boa
and the ginger fox biting its tail
to where my girl lies, waiting . . .
and we'll stay there, quiet,
until daylight finds us.

Parlor

We passed through
on the way to anywhere else.
No one lived there
but silence, a pale china gleam,

and the tired eyes of saints
aglow on velvet.

Mom says things are made
to be used. But Grandma insisted
peace was in what wasn't there,
strength in what was unsaid.

It would be nice to have a room
you couldn't enter, except in your mind.
I like to sit on my bed
plugged into my transistor radio,
"Moon River" pouring through my head.

How do you *use* life?
How do you *feel* it? Mom says

things harden with age; she says
Grandma is happier now. After the funeral,
I slipped off while they stood around
remembering—away from all
the talking and eating and weeping

to sneak a peek. She wasn't there.
Then I understood why
she had kept them just so:

so quiet and distant,
the things that she loved.

The First Book

1 Open it.

2 Go ahead, it won't bite.
3 Well . . . maybe a little.

4 More a nip, like. A tingle.
5 It's pleasurable, really.

6 You see, it keeps on opening.
7 You may fall in.

8 Sure, it's hard to get started;
9 remember learning to use

10 knife and fork? Dig in:
12 You'll never reach bottom.

13 It's not like it's the end of the world—
14 just the world as you think

15 you know it.

Maple Valley Branch Library, 1967

For a fifteen-year-old there was plenty
to do: Browse the magazines,
slip into the Adult Section to see
what vast *tristesse* was born of rush-hour traffic,
décolletés, and the plague of too much money.
There was so much to discover—how to
lay out a road, the language of flowers,
and the place of women in the tribe of Moost.
There were equations elegant as a French twist,
fractal geometry's unwinding maple leaf;

I could follow, step-by-step, the slow disclosure
of a pineapple Jell-O mold—or take
the path of Harold's purple crayon through
the bedroom window and onto a lavender
spill of stars. Oh, I could walk any aisle
and smell wisdom, put a hand out to touch
the rough curve of bound leather,
the harsh parchment of dreams.

As for the improbable librarian
with her salt and paprika upsweep,
her British accent and sweater clip
(mom of a kid I knew from school)—
I'd go up to her desk and ask for help
on bareback rodeo or binary codes,
phonics, Gestalt theory,
lead poisoning in the Late Roman Empire,
the play of light in Dutch Renaissance painting;
I would claim to be researching
pre-Columbian pottery or Chinese foot-binding,

but all I wanted to know was:
Tell me what you've read that keeps
that half smile afloat
above the collar of your impeccable blouse.

So I read *Gone with the Wind* because
it was big, and haiku because they were small.
I studied history for its rhapsody of dates,
lingered over Cubist art for the way
it showed all sides of a guitar at once.
All the time in the world was there, and sometimes
all the world on a single page.
As much as I could hold
on my plastic card's imprint I took,

greedily: six books, six volumes of bliss,
the stuff we humans are made of:
words and sighs and silence,
ink and whips, Brahma and cosine,
corsets and poetry and blood sugar levels—
I carried it home, past five blocks of aluminum siding
and the old garage where, on its boarded-up doors,
someone had scrawled:

I CAN EAT AN ELEPHANT
IF I TAKE SMALL BITES.

Yes, I said, to no one in particular: *That's*
what I'm gonna do!

Freedom: Bird's-Eye View

The sun flies over the madrigals,
outsmarting the magisterial
wits, sad ducks
who imagine they matter.
What a parade! Wind tucks
a Dixie cup up its
sleeve, absconds
with a kid's bright chatter
while above, hawks
wheel as the magistrates circle
below, clutching their hats.

I'm not buying. To watch
the tops of 10,000
heads floating by on sticks
and not care if one of them
sees me (though it
would be a kick!)
—now, that's
what I'd call
freedom,
and justice,
and ice cream for all.

Testimonial

Back when the earth was new
and heaven just a whisper,
back when the names of things
hadn't had time to stick;

back when the smallest breezes
melted summer into autumn,
when all the poplars quivered
sweetly in rank and file . . .

the world called, and I answered.
Each glance ignited to a gaze.
I caught my breath and called that life,
swooned between spoonfuls of lemon sorbet.

I was pirouette and flourish,
I was filigree and flame.
How could I count my blessings
when I didn't know their names?

Back when everything was still to come,
luck leaked out everywhere.
I gave my promise to the world,
and the world followed me here.

Dawn Revisited

Imagine you wake up
with a second chance: The blue jay
hawks his pretty wares
and the oak still stands, spreading
glorious shade. If you don't look back,

the future never happens.
How good to rise in sunlight,
in the prodigal smell of biscuits—
eggs and sausage on the grill.
The whole sky is yours

to write on, blown open
to a blank page. Come on,
shake a leg! You'll never know
who's down there, frying those eggs,
if you don't get up and see.

Black on a
Saturday Night

My Mother Enters the Work Force

The path to ABC Business School
was paid for by a lucky sign:
ALTERATIONS, QUALIFIED SEAMSTRESS INQUIRE WITHIN.
Tested on sleeves, hers
never puckered—puffed or sleek,
leg-o'-mutton or raglan—
they barely needed the damp cloth
to steam them perfect.

Those were the afternoons. Evenings
she took in piecework, the treadle machine
with its locomotive whir
traveling the lit path of the needle
through quicksand taffeta
or velvet deep as a forest.
And now and now sang the treadle,
I know, I know. . . .

And then it was day again, all morning
at the office machines, their clack and chatter
another journey—rougher,
that would go on forever
until she could break a hundred words
with no errors—ah, and then

no more postponed groceries,
and that blue pair of shoes!

Black on a Saturday Night

This is no place for lilac
or somebody on a trip
to themselves. Hips
are an asset here, and color
calculated to flash
lemon bronze cerise
in the course of a dip and turn.
Beauty's been caught lying
and the truth's rubbed raw:
Here, you get your remorse
as a constitutional right.

It's always what we don't
fear that happens, always
not now and why are
you people acting this way
(meaning we put in petunias
instead of hydrangeas and reject
ecru as a fashion statement).

But we can't do it—naw, because
the wages of living are sin
and the wages of sin are love
and the wages of love are pain
and the wages of pain are philosophy
and that leads definitely to an attitude
and an attitude will get you
nowhere fast so you might as well
keep dancing dancing till
tomorrow gives up with a shout,
'cause there is only

Saturday night, and we are in it—
black as black can,
black as black does,
not a concept
nor a percentage
but a natural law.

The Musician Talks about "Process"

(after Anthony "Spoons" Pough)

I learned the spoons from
my grandfather, who was blind.
Every day he'd go into the woods
'cause that was his thing.
He met all kinds of creatures,
birds and squirrels,
and while he was feeding them
he'd play the spoons,
and after they finished
they'd stay and listen.

When I go into Philly
on a Saturday night,
I don't need nothing but
my spoons and the music.
Laid out on my knees
they look so quiet,
but when I pick them up
I can play to anything:
a dripping faucet,
a tambourine,
fish shining in a creek.

A funny thing:
When my grandfather died,
every creature sang.
And when the men went out

to get him, they kept singing.
They sung for two days,
all the birds, all the animals.
That's when I left the South.

Sunday

Their father was a hunting man.
Each spring the Easter rabbit sprung open
above the bathroom sink, drip slowed
by the split pink pods of its ears
to an intravenous trickle.
There was the occasional deer,
though he had no particular taste
for venison—too stringy, he said,
but made Mother smoke it up just in case,
all four haunches and the ribs.

Summer always ended with a catfish
large as a grown man's thigh
severed at the hip, thrashing
in a tin washtub: a mean fish, a fish
who knew the world was to be endured
between mud and the shining hook.

He avoided easy quarry: possum
and squirrel, complacent carp.
He wouldn't be caught dead
bagging coon; coon, he said,
was fickle meat—tasted like
chicken one night, the next like
poor man's lobster. He'd never admit
being reduced to eating coon,
to be called out of his name
and into that cartoon.

It's not surprising they could eat the mess
he made of their playground: They watched
the October hog gutted with grim fury,

a kind of love gone wrong, but oh
they adored each whiskery hock, each
ham slice brushed subterranean green.

They were eating his misery
like bad medicine meant to help them
grow. They would have done anything
not to see his hand jerk like that,
his belt hissing through the loops and around
that fist working inside the coils
like an animal gnawing, an animal
who knows freedom's worth anything
you need to leave behind to get to it—
even your own flesh and blood.

The Camel Comes to Us
from the Barbarians

This one is enormous: rough-cut,
the fur like matted felt—
and so much of it,

rising in vulgar mounds upon its back
as if the sand itself had belched
into heaven's beard. Gods,

what malevolence! The eye a constant
rolling orb, glistening with ill intent,
yellowed, gummed with hair, more hairs

than you or I would care to count,
that eye marks every move its jailer makes
and waits for him to step too near—

one blow would cripple any man.
Another specimen stands bellowing
beneath the farthest palm. Though slighter,

it daunts equally, staked haunches
straining, muscles potent as the reek
that saturates our sun-baked marketplace.

About the larger one some purpose lurks:
Hindquarters splayed, it tugs against its ropes,
snorts, yearns its massive head and slavers

toward that godawful sound. Could
the drabber one be female, and its mate?
More monsters in our midst!

And yet . . . if these vile creatures be
like geese, or dogs, and their offspring
learn to cuddle the one

who coddles them first—why,
our fortune's pegged for sure.
Let us display our sternest countenance,

then apportion what they most desire
according to the measure of their service.
A rare commodity, these beasts—

who cannot know
what beauty wreaks, what mountains
pity moves.

The Venus of Willendorf

Let your eye be a candle in a chamber,
your gaze a knife;
let me be blind enough
to ignite it.
    —PAUL CELAN

She kneels on a workbench
strewn with clipper and trowel
to look out over the valley, red sun
still snagged on the farthest green fringe.
She's early. Behind her
scratch the arbor's last leaves
and a few gray birds pecking for crumbs
among the rose husks fallen to the veranda.

Arrived a week ago, one more exotic
in the stream of foreign students
invited to *Herr Professor*'s summer house
in the Wachau, she was taken
straight from train to tavern
to see the village miracle, unearthed
not five kilometers from this garden shed:

the legendary Venus of Willendorf.
Just a replica, *natürlich*,
a handful of primitive stone
entombed in a glass display
the innkeeper kept dusting as he told
his one story, charmed by the sight of
a live black girl. *Not five kilometers!*
he repeated, stopping his cloth

to reexamine the evidence:
sprawling buttocks and barbarous thighs,
breasts heaped up in her arms
to keep from spilling.
We should have kept her, he said.
Made the world come to us
here, in Austria.

                           "Here" seemed
hardly Austrian, although the Danube
had wandered through, scooped out a gorge
and left it clotted with poppies to dream
the haze of centuries away. Each morning
she heard children tumbling down the path
to catch the 7:10 on its milk run
to the school in Krems. Each evening
the Munich-Vienna express barreled through
at precisely—another miracle—
7:10.
          It was impossible, of course,
to walk the one asphalted street
without enduring a gauntlet of stares.
Have you seen her? they asked,
comparing her to their Venus
until she could feel her own breasts
settle and the ripening
predicament of hip and thigh.

They were on the veranda
when he confessed—no, "confided"
(wife occupied in the kitchen, slicing cake)
that his pubic hair had gone white.
She should have been shocked
but couldn't deny the thrill
it gave her, how her body felt

tender and fierce, all at once.
What made one sculpture so luscious
when there were real women, layered
in flesh no one worshipped?
The professor's wife, for instance,
hair too long and charred eyes
wild in their sockets as if to say
Where thou goest, there I went also—
no one devoured her with his glance as she
cleared away the tea things.

                           In Willendorf
twilight is brutal: no dim tottering
across flowery fields but blindness
dropped into the treeline like an ax.
He won't dare touch me,
she argues, *and risk destroying*
everything. Yet his gaze, glutting itself
until her contours blazed . . .
and suddenly she understands what made
the Venus beautiful
was how the carver's hand had loved her,
that visible caress.

                           Lightning
then a faint, agreeable thunder
as the express glides past below,
passengers snared in light, smudged flecks
floating in a string of golden cells.
If only we were ghosts, she thinks,
leaning into the rising hush,

if only I could wait forever.

Incarnation in Phoenix

Into this paradise of pain she strides
on the slim tether of a nurse's bell,
her charcoal limbs emerging from crisp whites
unlikely as an envelope issuing smoke.
I've rung because my breasts have risen,
artesian: I'm not ready for this motherhood stuff.

Her name is Raven. And she swoops
across the tiled wilderness, hair boiling
thunder over the rampart of bobby pins
spoking her immaculate cap. She dips once
for the baby just waking, fists punching
in for work "right on schedule"—
bends again to investigate what
should be natural, milk sighing into
one tiny, vociferous mouth. "Ah,"
she whispers, "ambrosia,"

shaming me instantly. But
no nectar trickles forth, no manna
descends from the vault of heaven
to feed this pearly syllable, this
package of leafy persuasion
dropped on our doorstep and ripening
before us, a miniature United Nations
"Just like me!" Raven says, citing

the name of her mother's village
somewhere in Norway, her father
a buffalo soldier. Now,
of course, we can place her:

an African Valkyrie
who takes my breast in her fists
grunting, "This hurts you more
than it does me"—then my laugh
squeezed to a whimper and the milk running out.

Revenant

Best Western Motor Lodge,
AAA Approved

Where can I find Moon Avenue,
just off Princess Lane? I wandered
the length of the Boulevard of the Spirits,
squandered a wad on Copper Queen Drive;

stood for a while at the public drinking fountain,
where a dog curled into his own hair
and a boy knelt, cursing his dirtied
tennis shoes. I tell you, if you feel strange,

strange things will happen to you:
Fallen peacocks on the library shelves
and all those maple trees, plastering
the sidewalks with leaves,

bloody palm prints everywhere.

Revenant

Palomino, horse of shadows.
Pale of the gyrfalcon
streaking free,
a reckoning—

the dark climbing out a crack in the earth.

Black veils starched for Easter.
The black hood of the condemned,
reeking with slobber.
The no color behind the eyelid
as the ax drops.

Gauze bandages over the wounds of State.

The canvas is primed, the morning
bitten off but too much to chew.
No angels here:
The last one slipped the room
while your head was turned,

made off for the winter streets.

On Veronica

*"I sat in front of the mirror, covered it over with
plastic and copied on it the outlines of my face."*
—EWA KURYLUK, *JOURNEY TO THE FRONTIERS OF ART*

Exposed to light,
the shroud lifts
its miraculous inscription—

a wound. Skin talking:
yes there, touch me there.
The stain of a glance,

a glance caught off-
guard, how it slices,
how each mirror imperils!

Or the acid sweat of sex,
cool ache of a breeze . . .
a hassock, stars.

Heaven encoded in the blue
volume of an arch
imploding,

shadows burned into doorways
at the zero point.
Dots and dashes.

The beloved's face
captured, rising from zero
onto the glistening plate—

white room, white sky.

There Came a Soul

After IVAN ALBRIGHT'S *Into the World There Came a Soul Called Ida*

She arrived as near to virginal
as girls got in those days—i.e., young,
the requisite dewy cheek
flushed at its own daring.
He had hoped for a little more edge.
But she held the newspaper rolled like a scepter,
his advertisement turned up to prove
she was there solely at his bidding—and yet
the gold band, the photographs . . . a mother, then.

He placed her in the old garden chair,
the same one he went to evenings
when the first tug on the cord sent the bulb
swinging like the lamps in the medic's tent
over the wounded, swaddled shapes that moaned
each time the Screaming Meemies let loose,
their calculated shrieks so far away
he thought of crickets—while all around him
matted gauze and ether pricked up
an itch so bad he could hardly sketch
each clean curve of tissue opening.
I shut my eyes, walk straight to it.
Nothing special but it's there, wicker
fraying under my calming fingers.

What if he changed the newspaper into a letter,
then ripped it up and tucked the best part

from view? How much he needed that desecrated
scrap! And the red comb snarled with a few
pale hairs for God in his infinite greed
to snatch upon like a hawk targeting a sparrow—
he couldn't say *At least I let you keep your hair*
so he kept to his task, applying paint
like a bandage to the open wound.

Pretty Ida, out to earn a penny
for her tiny brood.
He didn't mask the full lips
or the way all the niggling fears
of an adolescent century
shone through her hesitant eyes,
but he painted the room out, blackened
every casement, every canvas drying
along the wall, even the ailing coffeepot
whose dim brew she politely refused,
until she was seated
as he had been, dropped
bleak and thick,
onto the last chair in the world.

The Peach Orchard

What the soul needs, it uses.
—JAMES HILLMAN

I say there is no memory of him
staining my palms and my mouth.
I walk about, no longer human—
something shameful, something
that can't move at all.

Women invented misery,
but we don't understand it.
We hold it close and tell it
everything, cradle the ache
until it seeps in and he's

gone, just like the wind
when the air stands still.
I'll step lightly
along the path between
the blossoming trees,

lightly over petals
drifting speechless and pale.
No other story could have
brought me here: this
stone floor. And branches,

bank upon bank of them brimming
like a righteous mob, like
a ventriloquist humming,

his hand up
my spine . . . O these

trees, shedding all
over themselves.
Only a fool
would think such frenzy
beautiful.

Against Repose

(BALCONY, BERLIN, 1981)

Nothing comes to mind.

I place my arm on my knee
and a small ache shimmers
in the elbow. Gristle
perhaps, or the nub of a nerve.
Who knows? Don't think;
lean into the wrought iron
until the table quakes, sends the wine aquiver.

Nothing happens.
Red homunculus settling,
green—*Libelle?* cicada?—drifting by
as a breeze rouses the linden,
lifts a millimeter of leaf
all the way down the boulevard.
This elbow's no good. I'd rather be

anywhere—and if I dare blink
or belch, or scratch at my furrowed unease;
if I refuse to look up, into God's
bland countenance . . .
the lost wing would still itch
and the wine stay bitter
in the glass—a mouthful of sin

in an inchful of hell.

Against Self-Pity

It gets you nowhere but deeper into
your own shit—pure misery a luxury
one never learns to enjoy. There's always some

meatier malaise, a misalliance ripe
to burst: Soften the mouth to a smile and
it stutters; laugh, and your drink spills onto the wake

of repartee gone cold. Oh, you know
all the right things to say to yourself: Seize
the day, keep the faith, remember the children

starving in India . . . the same stuff
you say to your daughter
whenever a poked-out lip betrays

a less than noble constitution. (Not that
you'd consider actually *going* to India—all
those diseases and fervent eyes.) But if it's

not your collapsing line of credit, it's
the scream you let rip when a centipede
shrieks up the patio wall. And that

daughter? She'll find a reason to laugh
at you, her dear mother: *Poor thing*
wouldn't harm a soul! she'll say, as if

she knew of such things—
innocence, and a soul smart enough to know
when to get out of the way.

Götterdämmerung

A straw reed climbs the car antenna.

Beyond the tinted glass, golden waves
of grain. *Golly!* I can't help
exclaiming, and he smirks—
my born-again naturalist son
with his souped-up laptop,
dear prodigy who insists
on driving the two hours
to the jet he insists I take.
(No turboprops for this

old lady.) On good days
I feel a little meaty; on bad,
a few degrees from rancid.
(Damn knee: I used it this morning
to retrieve a spilled colander;
now every cell's blowing whistles.)

At least it's still a body.
He'd never believe it, son of mine,
but I remember what it's like
to walk the world
with no help from strangers,
not even a personal trainer
to make you feel the burn.

(Most of the time, it's flutter-heart
and Her Royal Celestial Mustache.
Most of the time I'm broth
instead of honey in the bag.)

So I wear cosmetics maliciously
now. And I like my bracelets,
even though they sound ridiculous,
clinking as I skulk through the mall,
store to store like some ancient
iron-clawed griffin—but I've never

stopped wanting to cross
the equator, or touch an elk's
horns, or sing *Tosca* or screw
James Dean in a field of wheat.
To hell with wisdom. They're all wrong:
I'll never be through with my life.

Ghost Walk

The neighbors who never
set foot in the castle
never tasted the truffles or château rosé
say she walks room to room
all night turning the lights on
and by day a cold wind blows
through the tiered gardens
pinching leaves from the withering rose

It is said in the village
she died of pure heartbreak
not a love turned away
but a love lasting only
as long as a lifetime
his life and no longer
not enough for the lady
hair red as a brushfire

that refused to go out
though it faded with years
to the orange of the coral
that lives in the sea
and still she was lovely
pale beauty became her
like pearls or a music box
like *Kaffee mit Schlag*

slim in an era when slim wasn't in fashion
she climbed into her tub
lined with bath salts and mirrors
chin-deep in scent
she would dream of a body
that could hold all of her
keep her afloat on this ocean
of good sense and breeding

she told no one not even
the one man she lived for
she put on her lipstick
she combed her brave hair
which she bore like a lantern
into the murmuring parlor
where they waited with smiles
and champagne on their lips

all night the waves pitching
all day the crows wheeling
through skies blue as his eyes
bright above the stunned lake
when he died she lay down
in their bed of silk tassels
in their bed of fringed curtains
and rose-colored satin

she lay down without tears
in that blushing cradle
and slept in that rocking
that cargo of sighs
each night the bed creaking
cast onto the waves
each dawn roses flaunting
their loose tongues of flame

she's a kind spirit
they assure us
down in the village
poor soul left behind
when the party was over
searching the rooms
for his laughter
and a last glass of wine

Lady Freedom Among Us

don't lower your eyes
or stare straight ahead to where
you think you ought to be going

don't mutter *oh no*
not another one
get a job   fly a kite
go bury a bone

with her oldfashioned sandals
with her leaden skirts
with her stained cheeks and whiskers and heaped up trinkets
she has risen among us in blunt reproach

she has fitted her hair under a hand-me-down cap
and spruced it up with feathers and stars
slung over one shoulder she bears
the rainbowed layers of charity and murmurs
all of you   even the least of you

don't cross to the other side of the square
don't think *another item to fit on a tourist's agenda*

consider her drenched gaze   her shining brow
she who has brought mercy back into the streets
and will not retire politely to the potter's field

having assumed the thick skin of this town
its gritted exhaust its sunscorch and blear
she rests in her weathered plumage
bigboned   resolute

don't think you can ever forget her
don't even try
she's not going to budge

no choice but to grant her space
crown her with sky
for she is one of the many
and she is each of us

For Sophie, Who'll Be
in First Grade in the Year 2000

No bright toy
this world we've left you.
Even the wrapping
is torn, the ribbons
grease-flecked and askew.
Still, it's all we have.

Wait a moment before
you pick it up. Study
its scratches, how it
shines in places. Now
love what you touch,
and you will touch wisely.

May the world, in your hands,
brighten with use. May you
sleep in sweet breath and
rise always in wonder
to mountain and forest,
green gaze and silk cheek—

dear Sophie,
littlest phoenix.

On the Bus with Rosa Parks

*All history is a negotiation
between familiarity and
strangeness.*

—SIMON SCHAMA

Sit Back, Relax

Lord, Lord. No rest
for the wicked?
Most likely no
heating pads.

*(Heat some gravy for the potatoes,
slice a little green pepper
into the pinto beans . . .)*

Sometimes a body
just plain grieves.

Stand by me in this, my hour—

"The situation is intolerable"

Intolerable: that civilized word.
Aren't we civilized, too? Shoes shined,
each starched cuff unyielding,
each dovegray pleated trouser leg
a righteous sword advancing
onto the field of battle
in the name of the Lord . . .

Hush, now. Assay
the terrain: all around us dark
and the perimeter in flames,
but the stars—
tiny, missionary stars—
on high, serene, studding
the inky brow of heaven.

So what if we were born up a creek
and knocked flat with the paddle,
if we ain't got a pot to piss in
and nowhere to put it if we did?
Our situation is intolerable, but what's worse
is to sit here and do nothing.
O yes. O mercy on our souls.

Freedom Ride

As if, after High Street
and the left turn onto Exchange,
the view would veer onto
someplace fresh: Curaçao,
or a mosque adrift on a milk-fed pond.
But there's just more cloud cover,
and germy air
condensing on the tinted glass,
and the little houses with
their fearful patches of yard
rushing into the flames.

Pull the cord a stop too soon, and
you'll find yourself walking
a gauntlet of stares.
Daydream, and you'll wake up
in the stale dark of a cinema,
Dallas playing its mistake over and over
until even that sad reel won't stay
stuck—there's still
Bobby and Malcolm and Memphis,
at every corner the same
scorched brick, darkened windows.

Make no mistake: There's fire
back where you came from, too.
Pick any stop: You can ride
into the afternoon singing with strangers,
or rush home to the scotch
you've been pouring all day—
but where you sit is where you'll be
when the fire hits.

Climbing In

Teeth.
Metallic. Lie-gapped.
Not a friendly shine

like the dime
cutting my palm
as I clutch the silver pole
to step up, up

(sweat gilding the dear lady's
cheek)—these are big teeth,
teeth of the wolf

under Grandmother's cap.
Not quite a grin.
Pay him to keep smiling

as the bright lady tumbles
head over tail
down the clinking gullet.

Claudette Colvin Goes to Work

Another Negro woman has been arrested and thrown into jail
because she refused to get up out of her seat on the bus and
give it to a white person. This is the second time since the
Claudette Colbert [sic] case. . . . This must be stopped.
—BOYCOTT FLIER, DECEMBER 5, 1955

Menial twilight sweeps the storefronts along Lexington
as the shadows arrive to take their places
among the scourge of the earth. Here and there
a fickle brilliance—lightbulbs coming on
in each narrow residence, the golden wattage
of bleak interiors announcing *Anyone home?*
or *I'm beat, bring me a beer.*

Mostly I say to myself *Still here.* Lay
my keys on the table, pack the perishables away
before flipping the switch. I like the sugary
look of things in bad light—one drop of sweat
is all it would take to dissolve an armchair pillow
into brocade residue. Sometimes I wait until
it's dark enough for my body to disappear;

then I know it's time to start out for work.
Along the Avenue, the cabs start up, heading
toward midtown; neon stutters into ecstasy
as the male integers light up their smokes and let loose
a stream of brave talk: "Hey Mama" souring quickly to
"Your Mama" when there's no answer—as if
the most injury they can do is insult the reason

you're here at all, walking in your whites
down to the stop so you can make a living.
So ugly, so fat, so dumb, so greasy—
What do we have to do to make God love us?
Mama was a maid; my daddy mowed lawns like a boy,
and I'm the crazy girl off the bus, the one
who wrote in class she was going to be President.

I take the Number 6 bus to the Lex Ave train
and then I'm there all night, adjusting the sheets,
emptying the pans. And I don't curse or spit
or kick and scratch like they say I did then.
I help those who can't help themselves,
I do what needs to be done . . . and I sleep
whenever sleep comes down on me.

The Enactment

*"I'm just a girl who people were mean to
on a bus. . . . I could have been anybody."*
—MARY WARE, NÉE SMITH

Can't use no teenager, especially
no poor black trash,
no matter what her parents do
to keep up a living. Can't use
anyone without sense enough
to bite their tongue.

It's gotta be a woman,
someone of standing:
preferably shy, preferably married.
And she's got to know
when the moment's right.
Stay polite, though her shoulder's
aching, bus driver
the same one threw her off
twelve years before.

Then all she's got to do is
sit there, quiet, till
the next moment finds her—and only then
can she open her mouth to ask
Why do you push us around?
and his answer: *I don't know but
the law is the law and you*

are under arrest.
She must sit there, and not smile
as they enter to carry her off;
she must know who to call
who will know whom else to call
to bail her out . . . and only then

can she stand up and exhale,
can she walk out the cell
and down the jail steps
into flashbulbs and
her employer's white
arms—and go home,
and sit down in the seat
we have prepared for her.

Rosa

How she sat there,
the time right inside a place
so wrong it was ready.

That trim name with
its dream of a bench
to rest on. Her sensible coat.

Doing nothing was the doing:
the clean flame of her gaze
carved by a camera flash.

How she stood up
when they bent down to retrieve
her purse. That courtesy.

QE2. Transatlantic Crossing. Third Day.

Panel of gray silk. Liquefied ashes. Dingy percale tugged over
the vast dim earth—ill-fitting, softened by eons of tossing
and turning, unfurling its excesses, recalling its losses,
no seam for the mending, no selvage to catch and align
from where I sit and look out from this rose-colored armchair
along the gallery. I can hear the chime of the elevator,

the hush of trod carpet. Beyond the alcove, escorted widows
perfect a slow rumba. Couples linger by the cocktail piano,
enmeshed in their own delight as others stroll past,
pause to remark on the weather. Mist, calm seas.
This is a journey for those who simply wish to be
on the way—to lie back and be rocked for a while, dangled

between the silver spoon and golden gate. Even
I'm thrilled, who never learned to wait on a corner,
hunched in bad weather, or how many coins to send
clicking into the glass bowl. I can only imagine
what it's like to climb the steel stairs and sit down, to feel
the weight of yourself sink into the moment of *going home.*

This is not the exalted fluorescence of the midnight route,
exhaustion sweetening the stops. There's
no money here, just chips and signatures,
no neat dime or tarnished token, no exact change.
Here I float on the lap of existence. Each night
I put this body into its sleeve of dark water with no more

than a teardrop of ecstasy, a thimbleful of ache.
And that, friends, is the difference—

I can't erase an ache I never had.
Not even my own grandmother would pity me;
instead she'd suck her teeth at the sorry sight
of some Negro actually looking for misery.

Well. I'd go home if I knew where to get off.

In the Lobby of the Warner Theatre, Washington, D.C.

They'd positioned her—two attendants flanking the wheelchair—
at the foot of the golden escalator, just right
of the movie director who had cajoled her to come.
Elegant in a high-strung way, a-twitch in his tux,
he shoved half spectacles up the nonexistent
bridge of his nose. Not that he was using her
to push his film, but it was only right (wasn't it?)
that she be wherever history was being made—after all,

she was the true inspiration, she was *living* history.
The audience descended in a cavalcade of murmuring
sequins. She waited. She knew how to abide,
to sit in cool contemplation of the expected.
She had learned to travel a crowd
bearing a smile we weren't sure we could bear
to receive, it was so calm a suturing.
Scrolling earthward, buffed bronze

in the reflected glow, we couldn't wait but leaned out
to catch a glimpse, and saw
that the smile was not practiced at all—
real delight bloomed there. She was curious;
she suffered our approach (the gush and coo,
the babbling, the director bending down
to meet the camera flash) until someone
tried to touch her, and then the attendants

pushed us back, gently. She nodded,
lifted a hand as if to console us
before letting it drop, slowly, to her lap.
Resting there. The idea of consolation
soothing us: her gesture
already become her touch,
like the history she made for us sitting there,
waiting for the moment to take her.

The Pond, Porch-View:
Six P.M., Early Spring

I sit, and sit, and will my thoughts
the way they used to wend
when thoughts were young
(i.e., accused of wandering).
The sunset ticks another notch
into the pressure treated rails
of the veranda. My heart, too,
has come down to earth;
I've missed the chance
to put things in reverse,
recapture childhood's backseat
universe. Where I'm at now
is more like riding on a bus
through unfamiliar neighborhoods—
chair in recline, the view chopped square
and dimming quick. I know
I vowed I'd get off
somewhere grand; like that dear goose
come honking down
from Canada, I tried to end up
anyplace but here.
Who am I kidding? Here I am.

Notes and Acknowledgments

Notes

"The Camel Comes to Us from the Barbarians": This allegorical poem was inspired by an Aesop fable entitled "The First Appearance of the Camel"; it relates how man's terror of this strange and powerful creature gradually turns to contempt once the means to control and domesticate the animal were discovered.

"There Came a Soul": Ivan Albright (1897–1983) began his painting of Ida Rogers in 1929. Although the model was a twenty-year-old wife and mother, the Chicago artist decided to portray her as a lonely old woman. Art scholars cite Albright's experience as a medical illustrator during World War I as a possible motive for his later preoccupation with old age.

"On the Bus with Rosa Parks": In 1995, during a convention in Williamsburg, Virginia, as the conferees were boarding buses to be driven to another site, my daughter leaned over and whispered, "Hey, we're on the bus with Rosa Parks!" Although the precipitating incident did not make it into a poem, the phrase haunted me—and so this meditation on history and the individual, image and essence was born. (By the way, Mrs. Parks took a seat in the front of the bus.)

"Claudette Colvin Goes to Work": Before Rosa Parks's historic refusal to move to the back of the bus in Montgomery, Alabama, on December 1, 1955, several other women had been arrested for violating that city's public transportation segregation laws. On March 2 of the same year, fifteen-year-old Claudette Colvin refused to yield her seat to white high school students. And on October 21, Mary Louise Smith was on her way home from a bad day when she was roused from daydreaming by an irate white passenger; she, too, did not vacate her seat voluntarily.

Acknowledgments

The poems in *On the Bus with Rosa Parks* first appeared in the following publications:

Agni Review: "Cameos"; *American Poetry Review*: "Best Western Motor Lodge, AAA Approved"; *The American Scholar*: "Maple Valley Branch Library, 1967"; *Callaloo*: "Dawn Revisited"; *Chelsea*: "The Musician Talks about 'Process'"; *Doubletake*: "Parlor"; *The Georgia Review*: "On Veronica"; *The Gettysburg Review*: "Ghost Walk", and "The Camel Comes to Us from the Barbarians"; *International Quarterly*: "I Cut My Finger Once on Purpose"; *Meridian*: "The Peach Orchard"; *The New Yorker*: "Incarnation in Phoenix"; *Parnassus*: "Against Repose" and "Götterdämmerung"; *Poetry*: "For Sophie, Who'll Be in First Grade in the Year 2000," "Testimonial," and "The Venus of Willendorf"; *Poetry Review* (U.K.): "Singsong"; *The Progressive*: "Black on a Saturday Night"; *Slate*: "Against Self-Pity," Revenant," and "Sunday"; *USA Weekend*: "Freedom, Bird's-Eye View" and "My Mother Enters the Work Force."

The title sequence, "On the Bus with Rosa Parks," was first published as a special section in *The Georgia Review*, Winter 1998.

"Lady Freedom Among Us" was read by the author at the ceremony commemorating the 200th anniversary of the United States Capitol and the restoration of the Statue of Freedom to the Capitol dome on October 23, 1993, and first published in the *Congressional Record* of the same day. It was subsequently commissioned as the four millionth volume of the University of Virginia Libraries in a fine press edition by Janus Press, West Burke, Vermont, 1994, and at the same time made globally accessible by the University of Virginia in a multimedia version on the Internet. "Lady Freedom Among Us" also appeared in *The Poet's World*, a volume of the author's poet laureate lectures at the Library of Congress (Library of Congress, 1995), and in several other publications.

"The First Book" appeared first in *The Language of Life*, ed. Bill Moyers, 1995. It is also available as an American Library Association poster and bookmark.

"There Came a Soul" appeared first in *Transforming Vision: Writers on Art*, ed. Edward Hirsch. The Art Institute of Chicago, 1994.

"Black on a Saturday Night" and "Singsong" (as "Song") are also part of *Seven for Luck*, a song cycle for soprano and orchestra, lyrics by Rita Dove, music by John

Williams, and appeared in the program for the song cycle's world premiere with the Boston Symphony Orchestra at Tanglewood July 25, 1998.

The epigraph to the title sequence is from Simon Schama's essay "Clio at the Multiplex," *The New Yorker,* January 19, 1998.

The author is grateful to the Rowohlt Foundation for a residency at Château de Lavigny, Switzerland, in 1996. Thanks are also due to the University of Virginia's Shannon Center for Advanced Studies, as well as to the Heinz Foundation for the 1996 John Heinz Award in the Arts and Humanities.

About the Author

RITA DOVE served as Poet Laureate of the United States from 1993 to 1995 and as Special Consultant for the Library of Congress bicentennial in 1999/2000. Born in 1952 in Akron, Ohio, she has published six poetry collections, among them *Thomas and Beulah*, which was awarded the Pulitzer Prize in 1987. She is also the author of the novel *Through the Ivory Gate* and the drama *The Darker Face of the Earth*, which premiered at the Oregon Shakespeare Festival in 1996 and was subsequently produced at the Kennedy Center in Washington, D.C., the Royal National Theatre in London, and other theaters. Her song cycle *Seven for Luck*, with music by John Williams, was first performed with the Boston Symphony at Tanglewood in 1998, and she collaborated with John Williams and Steven Spielberg for the White House Millennium production on New Year's Eve, 1999.

Dove's honors include Fulbright, Guggenheim, and Mellon fellowships, numerous honorary doctorates, the NAACP Great American Artist Award, *Glamour* magazine's "Woman of the Year' Award, the New York Public Library's "Literary Lion" citation, and the Golden Plate Award from the American Academy of Achievement, as well as residencies at Tuskegee Institute, the National Humanities Center, and the Rockefeller Foundation's Villa Serbelloni in Bellagio, Italy. Most recently she was the recipient of the Heinz Award, the National Humanities Medal, the Sara Lee Frontrunner Award, the Barnes & Noble Writers for Writers Award, and the Levinson Prize from *Poetry* magazine.

Dove is Commonwealth Professor of English at the University of Virginia in Charlottesville, where she lives with her husband, the German writer Fred Viebahn, and their daughter, Aviva.